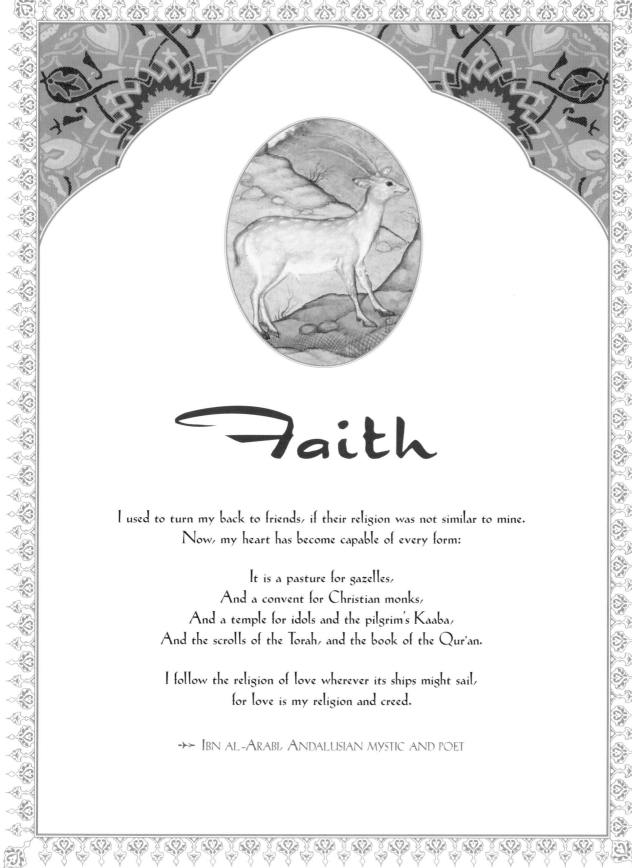

Faith

I used to turn my back to friends, if their religion was not similar to mine.
Now, my heart has become capable of every form:

It is a pasture for gazelles,
And a convent for Christian monks,
And a temple for idols and the pilgrim's Kaaba,
And the scrolls of the Torah, and the book of the Qur'an.

I follow the religion of love wherever its ships might sail,
for love is my religion and creed.

→→ IBN AL-ARABI, ANDALUSIAN MYSTIC AND POET

LIFE IN
THE MEDIEVAL MUSLIM WORLD

Faith

KATHRYN HINDS

MARSHALL CAVENDISH BENCHMARK NEW YORK

To Joyce

The author and publishers wish to extend heartfelt thanks to Dr. Josef W. Meri, Fellow and Special Scholar in Residence, Royal Aal al-Bayt Institute for Islamic Thought, Amman, Jordan, for his gracious and invaluable assistance in reviewing the manuscript.

MARSHALL CAVENDISH BENCHMARK 99 WHITE PLAINS ROAD TARRYTOWN, NEW YORK 10591 www.marshallcavendish.us Text copyright © 2009 by Marshall Cavendish Corporation. Map copyright © 2009 by Mike Reagan. All rights reserved. No part of this book may be reproduced or utilized in any form or by any means electronic or mechanical, including photocopying, recording, or by any information storage and retrieval system, without permission from the copyright holders. All Internet sites were available and accurate when this book was sent to press. LIBRARY OF CONGRESS CATALOGING-IN-PUBLICATION DATA Hinds, Kathryn, 1962- Faith / by Kathryn Hinds. p. cm. — (Life in the medieval Muslim world) Includes bibliographical references and index. Summary: "A social history of the Muslim world from the eighth through the mid-thirteenth century, with a focus on the religion of Islam"—Provided by publisher. ISBN 978-0-7614-3092-6 1. Islam—History. 2. Islam—Essence, genius, nature. 3. Islam—Customs and practices. 4. Islamic countries—Social life and customs. I. Title. BP50.H56 2009 297.09'02—dc22 2008019268

EDITOR: Joyce Needleman Stanton   PUBLISHER: Michelle Bisson
ART DIRECTOR: Anahid Hamparian   SERIES DESIGNER: Kristen Branch / Michael Nelson Design

Printed in China
135642

front cover: A man at the beginning of his prayers, painted by a European artist who visited Egypt several times in the 1800s
half-title page: A gazelle pictured in a manuscript from Muslim-ruled northern India
title page: Facing the direction of Mecca, men and boys from all walks of life pray together in a mosque.
back cover: This beautiful glass lamp, made in the 1300s, hung in a mosque in Egypt or Syria.

Contents

About the Medieval Muslim World

IN THE YEAR 622 AN ARABIAN MERCHANT NAMED Muhammad, accompanied by two hundred followers, left his home city of Mecca for the troubled town of Yathrib. Its citizens knew that Muhammad had been receiving visions from God and preaching what God had revealed to him. His message was unpopular in Mecca, but the people of Yathrib welcomed Muhammad to be their chief judge and embraced his teaching of Islam, or submission to God. They recognized Muhammad as the Prophet of God, and their city soon became known as Madinat al-Nabi, "City of the Prophet," or simply Medina.

The Hegira, Muhammad's move to Medina, marked the beginning of the Islamic community, the *umma*. From that point on, the community of Muslims (followers of Islam) grew rapidly. By 634 it embraced the entire Arabian Peninsula. By 750 Muslim rulers controlled a wide band of territory from the Iberian Peninsula, across North Africa, to the borders of India. During the following centuries the *umma* continued to expand into India, Anatolia (modern Turkey), Central Asia, and sub-Saharan Africa. Along the way, Arab and local

Opposite: Medina, the City of the Prophet, as it appeared on a moonlit night in 1918. The dome at the center covers Muhammad's tomb.

7

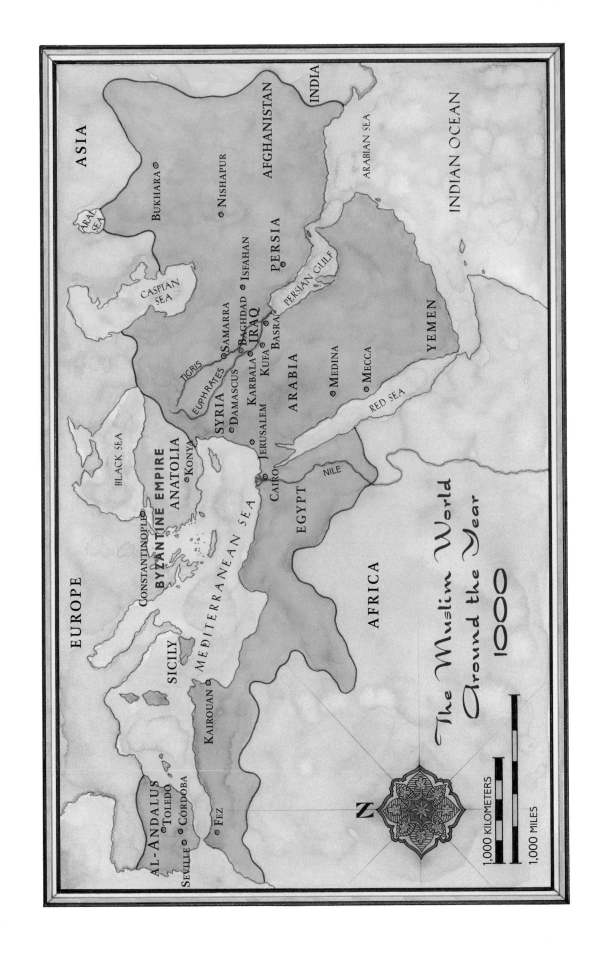

The Muslim World Around the Year 1000

cultures mingled and sometimes melded, leading to the development of a shared Muslim culture with many ways of expressing itself.

The Dar al-Islam, "Abode of Islam," was politically united for only a brief period. But it remained united in other important ways, through religious beliefs and language. Arabic, the language of the Qur'an (the holy book of Islam), became the common tongue of nearly all Muslims in Islam's early centuries. In most areas it was used not just in religion but also in government, law, literature, and learning. This meant that no matter where a Muslim went in the Dar al-Islam, he or she would be able to share news and knowledge with other Muslims. In fact the gathering, communication, and spreading of knowledge and skills in the arts and sciences was one of the great achievements of the Muslim world during this era. For this reason, it is sometimes referred to as the Golden Age of Islam. In the history of the West, this time is generally called the Middle Ages, and for convenience we use both that term and *medieval* for this period even when discussing areas outside Europe.

The Dar al-Islam and Christian medieval Europe often conflicted with each other. Yet there was also a great deal of peaceful interchange between the two, in many ways to the lasting benefit of European civilization. And at various times and places in the medieval Muslim world, Muslims, Christians, and Jews lived and worked side by side in an atmosphere of tolerance seldom found elsewhere in the past. In the present, too, we can find much to learn from both the successes and the struggles of the Dar al-Islam in the Middle Ages.

This series of books looks at the lives of the people who lived in that diverse world, focusing mainly on the Middle East and Spain in the eighth through thirteenth centuries. In this volume we will learn about the roles of faith in medieval Muslim life. We will meet mystics and scholars, judges and warriors, and ordinary women and

Noah's Ark, with horses, camels, and donkeys looking out the portholes. Noah belonged to the long line of prophets honored by Muslims.

men, visiting them in mosques, schools, hospitals, and homes. These people had many of the same joys and sorrows, hopes and fears that we do, but still their world was very different from ours. So step back into history, to a time of faith and intellect, intrigue and excitement, struggle and splendor. Welcome to life in the medieval Muslim world!

Faith

A NOTE ON DATES AND NAMES

For Muslims the Hegira (Arabic *hijra*, "departure" or "emigration") began a new age and so became the year 1 of the Muslim calendar. Dates in this calendar are labeled AH, for *Anno Hegira*, or simply H. For ease of reading, though, this series of books uses the conventional Western dating system. Also for ease of reading, we are using the common Westernized forms of many Arabic names—for example, *Avicenna* instead of *Ibn Sina*—and we are leaving out most of the special accent marks that scholars use when converting Arabic names to the Western alphabet. There are many different ways to convert Arabic to English, especially because the Arabic alphabet does not include symbols for most vowels. For this reason, you may see the same names spelled slightly different ways in different books. In many sources you may also see the God of Islam referred to as Allah. Since the Arabic word *Allah* simply means *God* and refers to the same deity worshipped by Jews and Christians, we have chosen to use *God* instead of *Allah* in this series.

Above: A doctor arrives just in time to assist a man bitten by a snake. This illustration comes from a thirteenth-century Arabic translation of an ancient Greek medical text.

ONE

The Prophet

There is no god but God and Muhammad is the messenger of God.

→→ THE *SHAHADA,* THE MUSLIM STATEMENT OF FAITH

SLAM IS ONE OF THE WORLD'S THREE MAJOR monotheistic religions, or religions that believe in only one God. The other two are Judaism and Christianity. Islam is the youngest of the three but in some ways, according to Muslim thought, it is the oldest—indeed, the original monotheism. For Muhammad, Islam was a return to the relationship with God that had been experienced by Abraham (regarded as the father of both the Hebrew and Arab peoples) and, earlier, by Noah and even Adam. Muhammad, and the Muslims who came after, honored these and other major figures of the Jewish scriptures (known by Christians as the Old Testament). Muslims also revered (and continue

Opposite: Relatives come to see the newborn Muhammad. He and his mother, Amina, are shown veiled so that people will not be tempted to worship their images.

Mary shakes dates out of a palm tree to feed herself and the baby Jesus (lying swaddled on the grass). The Arabic names for Mary and Jesus are Maryam and Isa.

to revere) Jesus; his mother, Mary; and John the Baptist from the Christian tradition. They, too, were members of the long line of prophets and holy people stretching back through time. For most Muslims, Muhammad was the last of this line, bringing humanity God's message in its most complete, perfect form.

MUHAMMAD'S EARLY LIFE

Muhammad was born in 570 in Mecca, Arabia's major city. He began life at a disadvantage, since his father had died seven months earlier—being fatherless would be not only an emotional hardship but would make his position in society uncertain and difficult right from the start. When he was six his mother died, and for the next two years he lived with his grandfather, whose death then left Muhammad not only orphaned but penniless—all of his grandfather's property was inherited by other family members.

Fortunately, Muhammad was taken in by the new head of their clan, or extended family group, his uncle Abu Talib. Abu Talib raised Muhammad with great care and kindness, and his other uncles also gave him assistance. One taught him archery and swordsmanship. When Muhammad was old enough, another uncle found him a job as a caravan guide.

Muhammad soon became known for his efficiency and trustworthiness. When he was twenty-five or so, a prosperous widowed businesswoman named Khadija hired him to lead a caravan to Syria and sell some goods for her there. The venture was a success, and Khadija was so impressed by Muhammad that she asked him to

marry her. They were very happy together and had four daughters. Their two sons, however, both died before the age of two. Muhammad freed and adopted one of his slaves to be his son, and he also took in his cousin Ali in order to help out Abu Talib, who was having difficulty supporting his large family. As Muhammad's own family grew, his reputation for fairness, honesty, and good judgment grew, too, and he was on his way to becoming one of Mecca's leading men.

The caravans Muhammad led would have been very much like this one carrying goods across the desert near the Red Sea in the 1800s.

THE MESSAGE

Around the age of thirty-five, Muhammad began going to a small cave outside the city to meditate during the month of Ramadan (the ninth month in the Arabian calendar). The cave was on a high hillside, and from its mouth Muhammad could look down to see the Kaaba, the holy place that was at the heart of Mecca. One night in the year 610, when Muhammad was forty years old, he had a startling, life-changing experience. Ibn Ishaq (died ca.

768), who wrote the first full biography of Muhammad, described what happened:

> When it was the night on which God honoured him with his mission and showed mercy on His servants thereby, [the angel] Gabriel brought him the command of God. "He came to me," said the apostle of God [Muhammad], "while I was asleep, with a coverlet of brocade whereon was some writing, and said, 'Read!' I said, 'What shall I read?' He pressed me with it so tightly that I thought it was death; then he let me go and said, 'Read!' [After this happened two more times,] I said, 'What then shall I read?'—and this I said only to deliver myself from him, lest he should do the same to me again. He said:
>
> > 'Recite in the name of thy Lord who created,
> > Who created man of blood coagulated.
> > Recite! Thy Lord is the most beneficent,
> > Who taught by [means of] the pen,
> > Taught that which they knew not unto men.'
>
> So I read it, and he departed from me. And I awoke from my sleep, and it was as though these words were written on my heart. . . ."

This Night of Power (or Destiny) marked the beginning of Muhammad's mission. But at first he was reluctant to accept it and feared that he was going insane or had been possessed by a jinni (a fiery nature spirit). Khadija and her Christian cousin reassured him, and soon he received divine reassurance in the form of another revelation: "By the pen and by that which they write. You [Muhammad] are not, by the grace of your Lord . . . possessed. Verily, yours is an unfailing reward."

Faith

After this, Muhammad began to share his revelations about Islam (submission to God) with his closest family and friends. Khadija was the first of them to embrace the new teaching, and the rest soon followed. Other spiritual seekers in Mecca, women and men of all classes, were attracted by the example of Muhammad and his followers, or Companions. Within three years there were thirty or forty Muslims, who met together to learn the divine messages that Muhammad continued to receive. Then Muhammad began to preach to other members of his clan and tribe.

The core of Muhammad's message was the oneness of God: "He is God, the One; God, the Absolute . . . and there is none like Him." Most Meccans, however, worshipped many gods, statues of which were housed in the Kaaba. This large cubical building was, in fact, a holy place that drew pilgrims from all over Arabia—a major reason for Mecca's importance and prosperity. So for both religious and economic reasons, Meccan leaders felt threatened by Islam.

A view from above of the Great Mosque of Mecca, depicted in an eighteenth-century Arabic manuscript. At the center is the Kaaba.

Moreover, Muhammad's revelations were full of teachings about caring for orphans, widows, the poor, and other disadvantaged people. The powerful were urged to be compassionate and charitable, and to accept responsibility for playing their part in bettering the entire community. These ideas displeased many of Mecca's proud and wealthy businessmen, who did not want to share their wealth with the less fortunate, in spite of the fact that generosity had long been a

The Prophet

core value among Arabia's tribes. Muhammad (or God speaking through Muhammad) also said that there would be a Judgment Day, and that those who had been cruel or unfeeling or unjust toward their fellow human beings would pay a price in the hereafter. To many Meccans, this idea seemed both ridiculous and offensive.

ENDINGS AND A NEW BEGINNING

The leaders of Mecca began to mock and insult the Muslims. Before long, harassment turned into threats and violence—some Muslims were beaten, tortured, or killed. For three years there was even a ban against marrying, trading, or making contracts with Muhammad or any member of his clan. Nothing, however, could succeed in ending Muhammad's preaching or the Muslims' dedication to their faith.

The year 619 brought the lifting of the ban, but it also brought great sorrow. First Khadija died, and then Abu Talib passed away. Without Khadija's support and Abu Talib's protection, Muhammad and his community were vulnerable to even more troubles. Muhammad began looking for ways to assure his people's safety. The solution came when representatives from the two major tribes of Yathrib, an oasis settlement about two hundred miles north of Mecca, invited Muhammad to help them put an end to their feuding and be their chief judge. A number of leading people in Yathrib had already become Muslims after contact with Muhammad and one of his students, and they promised to give their protection to the Meccan Muslims. So during the summer of 622, most of Muhammad's community moved from Mecca to Yathrib, soon to become known as Medina.

This emigration, the Hegira, marked a turning point. Earlier, Muhammad had believed his revelations were just for the Meccans.

Faith

But now it became clear that the message had equal meaning for people elsewhere. The joining of Meccan and Medinan Muslims marked the true beginning of a new community of believers, the *umma*. And as chief judge of Medina, Muhammad was able to start putting his ideals into wider practice. Many more Medinans embraced Islam, inspired by Muhammad's fairness and compassion and by the sincerity of the Muslims' faith. It seemed possible that the Prophet's vision of a more just society, united by love of God, was becoming a reality.

TWO

Scripture and Tradition

*O believers, believe in God and His Messenger and the Book He
has sent down on His Messenger. . . .*
↠ QUR'AN 4:136

A FTER THE NIGHT OF POWER, MUHAMMAD continued to receive revelations from God for more than twenty years. These divine messages came in different ways. They were often brought by Gabriel, who might appear to Muhammad in angelic form or as a human figure standing on the horizon. At other times the Prophet saw nothing but heard the revelation as clear words that fell on him like rain. And sometimes, Muhammad said, "it comes unto me like the reverberations of a bell, and that is the hardest upon me; the reverberations abate when I am aware of their message." He also said, "Never once did I receive a revelation without thinking that my soul had been torn away from me."

Opposite: The Qur'an was God's miraculous gift to believers. Each verse was regarded as a sign of God's greatness and mercy. This page comes from a Qur'an produced in Persia in the late 1100s. It was written out and decorated all by hand and with great care and devotion.

A Qur'an teacher helps his students understand the meaning of the sacred text. Ludwig Deutsch, a European artist, painted this scene in 1905 after several visits to Egypt.

THE QUR'AN

When Muhammad received a revelation, he committed it to memory immediately by reciting it—to the angel, to himself, and to his followers. His followers would then do the same, memorizing and reciting the revelations as they came, chapter by chapter, verse by verse. The revelations therefore were called the Qur'an, which means "recitation." Its verses were called *ayah*, "signs," for they were signs of God's greatness and mercy.

From the recitations, secretaries wrote down the revelations. Muslims who were literate read the Qur'an aloud to others, who could then memorize it to recite themselves. Few people in Arabia at this time were able to read, but books and literature were nevertheless held in great honor. Poetry was the highest art form, and Arabs in general had a strong appreciation for eloquence. The language of the Qur'an was very powerful and poetic, impressing some people so much that they converted immediately after hearing a recitation for the first time.

For most Muslims, the Qur'an was the pure, direct word of God. Because Arabic was the language God had chosen for these revelations, it was the language in which the Qur'an was always learned and recited. To this day, translations of the Qur'an into other languages are not regarded as truly the Qur'an—they are instead thought of as commentaries or interpretations of the scripture. The Qur'an's nature was so special that when Muhammad was asked to prove his prophethood by performing a miracle, he replied that the Qur'an itself was the miracle.

Muhammad's followers made sure the Qur'an was preserved and passed on, but it was not till the reign (644–656) of the Prophet's third successor, Uthman ibn Affan, that all the revelations were put together in a standard form. It was felt that God inspired the way the Qur'an was organized, with its chapters (called suras, meaning "steps") tending to be arranged with the longest near the beginning and the shortest toward the end. As a result the revelations were not in the same order that Muhammad received them, and each chapter might deal with many different subjects. But a Muslim could open the book and start reciting at any point, always finding food for thought or guidance to follow.

The Qur'an often gave strong, clear guidelines for human behavior. Good works, for instance, included "to free a slave, to feed the destitute on a day of hunger, [or to feed] a kinsman, orphan, or a stranger out of luck, in need." Such teachings were general and could apply to anyone at any time. Some revelations, however, dealt with particular situations or were given in response to specific concerns that Muhammad asked God for help with.

For example, some verses that spoke negatively about Jews were referring to Jewish tribes in Medina that had broken treaties with Muhammad. The problem was the tribes' betrayal and hostility, not their religion. Elsewhere the Qur'an was very clear about the respect due to Jews, as well as Christians, who after all had received their own sacred texts and teachings from the same God: "There is no god but Him, the Living, the Supporter of all. It is He who sent down to you step by step, in truth, the Book [the Qur'an], confirming what went before it; and He sent down the Torah and the Gospel before this, as a guide to humankind."

IN THE PROPHET'S FOOTSTEPS

During Muhammad's lifetime he was the main interpreter of the sacred text, and he could sort out any confusion about its meaning. But after his death, people still needed guidance to understand the scripture. This was especially true as times changed and the *umma* expanded into new lands and encountered cultures very different from that of seventh-century Arabia. Scholars worked hard to learn all they could about the Qur'an, its language, the events surrounding the revelations, and so on. One of the most important keys to understanding the Qur'an was Muhammad's own life.

The Qur'an told Muslims, "You have indeed in the Messenger of God an excellent example for the person who hopes in God and the Final Day, and who remembers God intensely." Muhammad was regarded as being as close to perfect as a human being could get, even in the way he learned from and corrected his mistakes. His words and deeds were looked on as the best guide, next to the Qur'an, for living the life of surrender to God.

In fact, Muhammad was sometimes thought of as "the living Qur'an," whose life expressed the workings of God's will. Aisha (pronounced *ah-EE-shah*), one of the wives Muhammad married after Khadija's death, said, "His character was the Qur'an." But although his example should be followed, he should never be worshipped. He

CONVERTED BY BEAUTY

There are many stories of people who embraced Islam because of the beauty of the Qur'an. One of the most famous is about a powerful Meccan named Umar ibn al-Khattab. Umar believed Muhammad was a dangerous troublemaker, so he decided to kill him. One of the Muslims, however, learned what Umar intended to do. He distracted him from his plan with the news that Umar's own sister, Fatima, and her husband were Muslims.

Muhammad often went to the Kaaba to pray and recite the Qur'an.

Umar immediately ran to Fatima's house, where she and her family were reading the Qur'an aloud. Umar burst in, demanding to know what they had been reciting. They refused to answer, which made him even angrier. He was about to hit his brother-in-law, but Fatima jumped in front of him so that Umar hit her instead. Fatima declared, "Yes, indeed, we are Muslims and we believe in God and His Messenger. As for you, you can now do as you please!"

After a moment Umar, shocked that he had struck his sister, asked Fatima to show him the text she had been reading. She made him wash his hands before handing him the pages, and then he began to read, "We have not sent down the Qur'an to you to [cause] your distress, but only as an admonition for those who fear [God]. A Revelation from Him who created the earth and the heavens on high." As Umar continued, he was struck by the scripture's beauty, which seemed to surpass the greatest Arab poetry: "How fine and noble is this speech!" He ran from Fatima's house to Muhammad's. As soon as he saw the Prophet, he exclaimed, "I have come to you to believe in God and his apostle and what he has brought from God."

In a different telling of Umar's conversion, he came upon Muhammad quietly reciting the Qur'an at the Kaaba one evening. Muhammad was alone and vulnerable, but Umar decided to hide and listen to him for a bit. Then, "When I heard the Qur'an, my heart was softened and I wept, and Islam entered into me." Whatever the exact circumstances of Umar's conversion, afterward he was one of Muhammad's staunchest supporters, and he eventually became the second caliph, one of the Prophet's successors in leading the *umma*.

always directed people to focus on God alone: "I am but a man like yourselves; the inspiration has come to me that your God is One God."

Muhammad's actions and habits were known as his Sunna ("trodden path" or "practice"). The Sunna set the pattern for the way Muslims should live. Religious people looked to Muhammad as a role model in all areas of life, showing them how to pray, how to handle disagreements, how to do business, how to raise a family, how to treat animals, how to wage war, how to bury the dead, and so on. At the heart of the Sunna were the hadiths ("reports"), statements by and about the Prophet that were remembered and passed on by his family and followers. These, too, dealt with all aspects of life, from the very spiritual to the very practical.

The Five Pillars

One of the most famous and important hadiths set forth the religious practices expected of all adult Muslims: "Islam has been built on five [pillars]: testifying that there is no god but God and that Muhammad is the Messenger of God, performing the prayers, paying the *zakat*, making the pilgrimage to the House [the Kaaba], and fasting in Ramadan." The first pillar refers to the *shahada*, the Muslim statement of faith (quoted at the beginning of chapter 1). A person became a Muslim by speaking the *shahada*, and continued to hear and say it every day afterward. It was part of the call to prayer and was repeated again at the end of prayers.

Prayer, or *salat*, the second pillar, took place five times a day: early morning, noon, midafternoon, sunset, and after dark (but before midnight). Muslims were naturally free to say their own personal prayers whenever they liked. *Salat*, however, was more formal, and it was the prayer of the entire community. During *salat* Muslims went through a series of Qur'an recitations, set prayers, and movements,

A page from a collection of Muhammad's sayings copied out around 1500 by a celebrated Turkish calligrapher, Shaykh Hamdullah of Amasya

HADITHS

During the early centuries of Islam, scholars put together authoritative collections of thousands of hadiths. Here are just a few of Muhammad's sayings from these collections:

"A strong man is a man who controls himself when he is angry."

"Moderation, moderation! For only with moderation will you succeed."

"God is gentle and he loves gentleness in everything."

"The best among you is the [one who is] best toward people."

"God is beautiful and he loves beauty."

"Verily there are heavenly rewards for any act of kindness to animals."

following the pattern established by the Prophet. For some parts of *salat* the worshippers stood, for others they bowed, and for others they knelt and touched their foreheads and hands to the ground.* This posture was called a prostration and was a physical expression of humbleness before God. It also showed that in the sight of God, all Muslims were equal.

The third pillar, *zakat*, was a tax that every financially able Muslim paid "for the poor and the destitute, for those that are engaged in the management of alms and those whose hearts are sympathetic to the Faith, for the freeing of slaves and debtors, for the advancement of God's cause, and for the traveler in need."

*People who had severe arthritis or other physical difficulties were required to perform only the postures that they were able to do, in keeping with the compassion taught by Muhammad.

Men at prayer in Cairo, each moving through the different postures at his own pace. This scene was painted by French artist Jean-Léon Gérôme after visiting Egypt in the mid-1800s.

Along with funding these good works, the *zakat* served to remind the rich to be grateful to God for their wealth and to remember they had a duty to help the less fortunate. Sometimes *zakat* was collected by religious officials, sometimes by the government, and sometimes people simply gave the money directly to those in need.

The fourth pillar was fasting during Ramadan, the month in which Muhammad received his first revelation. Every day from sunrise till dark, all healthy adult Muslims were expected to go without food or drink—even water. The Qur'an, however, took into account circumstances that might prevent people from fasting: "If any one among you is ill or on a journey, let him fast a similar number of days later; and for those that cannot endure it there is a ransom: the feeding of a poor man. . . . God desires your well-being, not your discomfort."

Pilgrims at the Kaaba, dressed in the simple white garments traditionally worn for the hajj, to emphasize the equality of all people before God

The pilgrimage to Mecca, or hajj, was the fifth pillar, and was something that should be done at least once by every Muslim who was physically and financially able. In the last year of his life, 632, Muhammad set the pattern for the hajj, which was based on the ancient Arabian pilgrimage to the Kaaba. Muhammad gave the traditional pilgrimage customs new religious meanings, largely in memory of Abraham, the founder of pure monotheism and ancestor of the Arabs.

The hajj was a formal event that took place over six days in the last month of the Muslim year. It involved a number of rituals and ceremonies, beginning at the Kaaba, believed to be the House of God built by Abraham and his son Ishmael (in Arabic, Ibrahim and Ismail). After circling the Kaaba seven times, pilgrims ran back and forth between two hills seven times. As they ran, they remembered how when Ishmael was a baby, he and his mother were banished and wandered in the wilderness, searching frantically for water. God did not let them die of thirst, however, but caused a spring to well up. It was known as Zamzam, and all pilgrims drank from it.

Another important part of the hajj took place in the desert on the Plain of Arafat, where the pilgrims stood from noon till sunset, praying and listening to sermons. This was where Adam had made submission to God, and was also where Muhammad had preached his last sermon. At a place called Mina, pilgrims threw rocks at three stone pillars, symbolizing their struggles against temptation, just as Abraham had struggled when God tested his faith.

Faith

An angel brings the ram for sacrifice to Ibrahim and Ismail (Abraham and Ishmael), rewarding the father and son for their unfailing faith in God.

The climax of the hajj commemorated the time that God asked Abraham to sacrifice Ishmael, as related in the Qur'an:*

And when they had both submitted to God's will, and Abraham had laid down his son prostrate upon his face, [God] called out to him, saying: "Abraham, you have fulfilled your vision." Thus [does God] reward the righteous. That was indeed a bitter test. [The Lord] ransomed his son with a noble sacrifice [God provided a ram to sacrifice instead] and bestowed on him the praise of later generations. "Peace be upon Abraham!"

In memory of this, pilgrims shaved their heads or cut off some of their hair, and then sacrificed a goat, sheep, or camel. They ate only a little of the meat themselves, and gave the rest to the poor. At the same time, people throughout the rest of the Muslim world celebrated the Feast of Sacrifice in solidarity with the pilgrims. Like so many other forms of Muslim worship, this feast expressed not only each Muslim's personal submission to God but also the strength and unity of the *umma*.

*In the Bible a similar story was told, but about Abraham's other son, Isaac (Genesis 22: 1–13).

Scripture and Tradition

THREE

The Community of Believers

*Know ye that every Muslim is a brother unto every other Muslim,
and that ye are now one brotherhood.*

➤➤ MUHAMMAD'S FAREWELL SERMON, DELIVERED DURING THE HAJJ IN 632

OR THE FIRST EIGHT YEARS AFTER MUHAMMAD'S move to Medina, the *umma* had to continually fight for its survival. But even as Mecca remained hostile, the Muslims were gaining converts and allies from many Arabian tribes. Finally, in 630, Muhammad led an army to Mecca, which surrendered without bloodshed. The Muslim forces entered the city peacefully, harming neither people nor property. Every enemy who asked for pardon received it, and Muhammad required no one to convert to Islam. Many people did convert, however, so impressed were they by the conduct of the Prophet and his followers. With peace assured, Muhammad left the city's leaders in place and returned to

Opposite: Accompanied by angels and his faithful companions, Muhammad makes his victorious return to Mecca.

Medina. By the time he died two years later, nearly all the Arabian tribes had embraced Islam or become allies of the *umma*.

THE SPREAD OF ISLAM

Warfare had long been a part of Arabian life—it was common, especially in times of hardship, for warriors from one tribe to raid another tribe for livestock, goods, and prisoners who could be held for ransom. This was all part of earning a living in the harsh desert environment of Arabia. Muhammad, however, had promoted peace among the various tribes, and so Muslims were forbidden to raid other Muslims or their allies. From the point of view of the time, for some, this was the one drawback of the unity that Islam had brought to the Arabian Peninsula.

But this unity also gave the Arabs newfound strength—and at a period when the neighboring Byzantine and Sasanian empires were weak and disorganized. To the Arabs it made good sense to raid the nearby non-Muslim lands, now so temptingly vulnerable. As the Arabs ventured farther and farther, their campaigns began to last too long for them to be able to return home between raids. Moreover, they found themselves in control of many of the lands they'd been plundering. So they built and settled down in garrison towns, such as Basra and Kufa (now Najaf) in Iraq, and Fustat (now Cairo) in Egypt. From these bases of operation, they governed the surrounding countryside.

The Muslim Arabs had become conquerors. By 641 Iraq, Syria, and Egypt were fully under their control. By 656 they had added Persia and much of North Africa to their domain. By 715 or so they had the whole southern Mediterranean and Middle East, from the Iberian Peninsula to the borders of India. In all of these places they left most of the land in the hands of the people who were already

Faith

there. The conquered became *dhimmis*, subjects who were under Muslim protection.

The Arabs did not wage war in order to spread Islam. But where they went, they naturally took their faith with them. At first they did not expect this faith to be embraced by the people they conquered—in fact, non-Arabs were actively discouraged from coverting, and there seemed to be little reason for them to do so. As Christians, Jews, or Zoroastrians (also called Magians), the *dhimmis* were "People of the Book"—people who had received their own revelations and scriptures.* It was this fact that gave them their protected position under Muslim rule, in keeping with the Qur'an's instructions:

A Bible scene, one of the many rich illustrations in a Haggadah from fourteenth-century Spain, where Jewish culture flourished under Muslim rule. This small book contained hymns, scripture readings, and other texts for use during Passover. Some of the pages are stained with wine, showing that the Haggadah enjoyed much use during Passover meals.

> Do not argue with the followers of earlier revelation otherwise than in a most kindly manner—unless it be such of them as are bent on evil-doing—and say: "We believe in that which has been bestowed from on high upon us, as well as that which has been bestowed upon you; for our God and your God is one and the same, and it is unto Him that we [all] surrender ourselves."

People in the conquered lands nevertheless converted to Islam in large numbers over the years. By the mid-800s Muslims made up more than half the population of the Middle East, and that majority continued to increase in size. Scholars estimate that in

*Later, when Hindus and Buddhists came under Muslim rule, they, too, were given *dhimmi* status.

A man at prayer, filled with love of God. The flames surrounding his head are a sign of holiness.

al-Andalus (Muslim-ruled Spain) the Muslim population grew from about 10 percent in the year 800 to at least 80 percent in 1000. Nearly all the converts made their choice freely—as the Qur'an said, "There shall be no coercion in matters of faith."

Not all converts embraced Islam purely out of faith, however. For some it was a practical, economic choice, since *dhimmis* had to pay an annual tax called the *jizya*. There were also restrictions on the activities of *dhimmis* (sometimes strongly enforced, sometimes not), which may have persuaded some that life would be easier as Muslims. For slaves and prisoners of war, conversion to Islam could win them their freedom, since a Muslim was forbidden to hold another Muslim in slavery. And many people, particularly in al-Andalus, seem to have embraced the new religion because they fell in love with the richness and refinement of Islamic culture.

DIFFERENT PATHS

Under Muhammad, the *umma* had been one united community, and the leaders who succeeded him—the caliphs—tried to keep it that way for as long as they could. But the seeds of division were sown right after the Prophet died. Although he had made no arrangement for a successor, much of the *umma* thought the natural choice was his cousin, Ali. Kinship ties were highly valued in Arabia, and Ali was not only Muhammad's closest living male relative but was also married to

Faith

his daughter Fatima. Medina's council of elders, however, felt Ali was not yet ready for the responsibilities of leadership. Instead they elected Abu Bakr, one of Muhammad's oldest friends and earliest Companions, as the first caliph.

The next two caliphs were also prominent Companions, Umar ibn al-Khattab and Uthman ibn Affan. Then in 656 a group of mutinying soldiers killed Uthman and proclaimed Ali caliph. Despite the circumstances, many

Muhammad blesses the marriage of his daughter Fatima and his cousin Ali. Fatima, like her father, is shown veiled.

Muslims felt that Ali was a good choice at this time. But others, led by the Prophet's widow Aisha, were angry that Ali did nothing to punish Uthman's assassins. Resentments boiled up on both sides, and civil war erupted. Ali defeated Aisha's forces, but his reign was never secure, and in 661 he was murdered.

Ali's supporters—his *shia*, or faction—had deeply resented the first three caliphs, whom they felt had taken Ali's rightful place. They were no happier with Ali's successor, who was Uthman's nephew Mu'awiya. When Mu'awiya's son Yazid became the next caliph, the *shia* protested that the caliphate belonged to Ali's son Husayn. Another civil war followed, in which Husayn and most of his family were killed at Karbala, Iraq.

The death of Husayn, the Prophet's grandson, was a tragic blow to the supporters of Ali and his family. As a result, their *shia* permanently

broke away from the rest of the *umma*, forming the Shi'i (or Shiite) branch of Islam. Shi'is believed that only descendants of Muhammad, through Ali, could rightfully lead the *umma* because only they inherited his inner spiritual power. Although this did not make them prophets, it did, according to Shi'i belief, qualify them as the best interpreters of the Qur'an and the laws based on it. Indeed, the Imams, as Shi'is called the leaders descended from Muhammad, were held to be infallible teachers when it came to religious matters.

By the late ninth century, one group of Shi'is, known as Twelvers, taught that there had been twelve Imams. The other main Shi'i group,

Scenes from before, during, and after the Battle of Karbala, combined in a painting by early twentieth-century Iranian artist Abbas al-Musavi. The death of Husayn can still inspire great emotion among Shi'i Muslims.

called Ismailis or Seveners, believed that the line had ended with the seventh Imam (whose name had been Ismail). In both cases, though, it was said that the last Imam had not died but had gone into a kind of mystical concealment. When Judgment Day approached, he would return as the Mahdi ("expected one"), who would reward his loyal followers and establish a perfect Islamic society.

Shi'is did not recognize the authority of the caliphs, especially in religious matters, and during the Middle Ages they rejected most political authority and involvement. When the caliphs weakened and became mainly figureheads, though, parts of the Dar al-Islam

The Community of Believers

did come under Shi'i rule, most notably the Buyid Dynasty in Persia and Iraq (934–1062) and the Fatimid Dynasty in North Africa, Egypt, and Syria (909–1171).

The main body of Muslims came to be known as Sunnis, from *ahl al-sunnah wa'l-jama'ah*, "followers of the Sunna and the majority." Another group, called the Kharijites ("seceders") felt that both Sunnis and Shi'is had shown themselves to be untrue to Muslim principles. The Kharijites took the Qur'an's instruction to "enjoin* good and forbid evil" in a strict sense, believing that everything—every action, every belief, every person—was either good or evil, with nothing in between. To the Kharijites, only a truly pure Muslim was worthy to lead the *umma* in its on-going fight against evil. Kharijites were always a small minority, but now and then during the Middle Ages, a ruler or dynasty or group of scholars would promote similar fundamentalist views.

Mystical Islam

Another group who sought to follow what they felt was the purest form of Islam were the Sufis. Their name probably came from the Arabic word for wool, because they dressed in rough woolen garments similar to those Muhammad had worn. Sufis tried to follow the Prophet's example by setting aside their selfish desires and living simple lives devoted to God.

Sufism arose as the Dar al-Islam expanded and its rulers became more and more wealthy and powerful. The upper classes developed a taste for luxury, and the merchants who satisfied this taste prospered in turn. The rich got richer, while the poor stayed poor. The early Sufis looked at their society and felt it was straying from Muhammad's ideals of equality, social justice, and plain living; Muslim leaders had

*command, promote, encourage

become too worldly and were losing sight of the true, spiritual message of the Qur'an. Hasan al-Basri (643–728), one of the first Sufi masters, wrote, "The lower (material) world is a house whose inmates labor for loss, and only abstention from it makes one happy in it. . . . For this world has neither worth nor weight with God, so slight it is."

In addition to turning their backs on such worldly concerns as wealth and power, Sufis were mystics. They sought to fully open their spirits to God, to experience his presence, and to lose themselves in his love. Sufism took as one of its major inspirations a certain category of hadiths known as sacred sayings, words that God spoke through Muhammad in addition to the revelations recorded in the Qur'an. One of these sayings in particular defined the Sufis' goal of *ihsan*, spiritual virtue or excellence: "*Ihsan* is that thou adorest God as though thou didst see Him, and if thou seest Him not, He nonetheless seeth thee."

Sufis were mainly from Sunni backgrounds. Many Sufis, however, tried to rise above the divisions within the *umma*—and within humanity as a whole. They tended to recognize a variety of ways of loving and submitting to God. Sufis often traveled widely, and their teaching and preaching inspired a large number of conversions to Islam—Sufis seemed to know how to speak of God and Islam in ways that people from diverse cultures and walks of life could understand and embrace. Taking the oneness of God as a pattern for their lives, Sufis believed, as the Qur'an said, "Wheresoever ye turn, there is the face of [God]."

Many Sufis embraced a life of absolute simplicity so that they could keep all their thoughts and actions focused on God.

Architects and artisans throughout the Muslim world have drawn on all their skills to honor God with beautiful houses of prayer. This image of the Blue Mosque, built in the early 1600s in Constantinople, was painted by twentieth-century English artist Lucy Willis.

FOUR

The Mosque

God builds a house in Paradise for him who builds a mosque.

→ A SAYING OF MUHAMMAD

THE ARABIC WORD *MASJID*, WHICH WE TRANSLATE as "mosque," literally means "a place of prostration"—a place to bow down before God in prayer. Muslims could pray anywhere: at home, at work, in the fields, in the marketplace, or wherever else they happened to be when they felt the need to communicate with God or heard the call to prayer. As Muhammad had said, "The whole earth is a *masjid*, a mosque." Nevertheless, Muslims have had special buildings in which to pray and worship since almost the beginning of the *umma*.

A PLACE OF PRAYER

The first mosque built by Muhammad in Medina was a very simple structure: a large rectangular space with a roof of palm fronds held up by tree trunks. When Muhammad preached, he stood on a stump or a stool. A rock marked the direction to face while praying—from 623 on, Muslims always prayed toward Mecca, the place where God had given Muhammad his first revelations.* In front of the mosque was a courtyard where community members could gather and where poor people could come to rest or receive food and other help. Muhammad and his wives lived in a group of huts surrounding the courtyard.

After the mosque was built, Muhammad wanted a way to call people to prayer, and considered ringing a bell as Christians did or blowing a shofar, or ram's horn, as Jews did on some holy days. Then one of the Medinan Muslims had a dream that gave Muhammad the answer: someone with a loud and beautiful voice should go up to a rooftop near the mosque and announce the time of *salat*. Muhammad chose a man named Bilal, a former slave from Abyssinia (now Ethiopia), who chanted the call to prayer that Muslims have answered ever since.

Muhammad's mosque in Medina was the model for other mosques, with the basic elements of prayer hall and courtyard. As the *umma* expanded and grew wealthier, however, the simple pattern was elaborated on to create much grander buildings. Starting in the 660s, tall towers called minarets were often built next to mosques. Minarets were used by the muezzins, the

Muezzins chant the call to prayer, their voices carrying out over the streets of Cairo.

*Before this, in Islam's early years, Muslims prayed facing Jerusalem.

Faith

44

men who chanted the call to prayer, and sometimes also served as lighthouses, watchtowers, and victory monuments. Rising high above the other buildings in a city, they could be very impressive.

Mosques were often beautifully decorated inside, with patterned brickwork, different colors of marble, sculpted plaster, intricate mosaics, or richly colored tiles. The decorations included geometric and abstract designs, calligraphy of hadiths and verses from the Qur'an, and sometimes images of plants, landscapes, and buildings. There were never images of people or animals, however, in order to keep worshippers from being tempted to associate other living beings with God. Usually the most beautifully decorated part of a mosque was the *mihrab*, sometimes called a prayer niche. This was an arch built into a wall to show the direction of Mecca. To many Muslims, it also symbolized a doorway into the spiritual world.

Another symbolic element that came to be important was the mosque lamp, which recalled this verse from the Qur'an:

God is the Light of the heavens and the earth;
the likeness of His light is as a niche
wherein is a lamp
(the lamp in a glass,
the glass as it were a glittering star). . . .

In a large mosque there could be hundreds of lamps hanging from the ceiling, looking like stars in the sky. Many mosques also drew worshippers' thoughts to heaven by roofing the area in front of the *mihrab* with a lofty dome.

A community's main mosque was known as the Friday mosque, because all Muslim men were expected to gather together here for the noon prayer every Friday. This prayer service also included a

This mosque scene painted by Jean-Léon Gérôme features a beautifully carved and painted *minbar*, or pulpit, which would be used by a preacher to deliver the Friday sermon.

sermon, so the mosque would have a tall pulpit for the preacher to stand in. Called a *minbar*, this pulpit was placed to the right of the *mihrab*. The *minbar* could be very ornate, carved from stone or made of wood inlaid with ivory, mother-of-pearl, or other rich materials. Friday crowds could number in the thousands, so worshippers generally filled the courtyard as well as the prayer hall.

Mosques often had fountains because, if at all possible, a Muslim always washed before praying. A hadith explained the symbolism and intention of this act: "When a believer performs ablutions and washes his face, all the sins he has committed with his eyes are washed away; when he washes his hands, all the sins he has committed with his hands are washed away; when he washes his feet, all the sins toward which he has stepped are washed away."

Faith

Some mosques had not just fountains but also attached bathhouses. As time went on, mosques added more and more facilities to meet the many needs of the *umma*.

COMMUNITY CENTERS

When Muhammad set up his mosque in Medina, he did not separate religious from social functions. He and his wives lived there; his grandchildren and their friends played there; he let travelers and beggars stay there; he and his Companions planned political and military strategies there. He did not want the place of prayer to be removed from the rest of the community—instead he wanted it to be the center of community life in every way.

The ceiling of the *mihrab*, or prayer niche, of the Great Mosque of Córdoba. The rich, intricate mosaics that decorate the *mihrab* were probably made by Byzantine craftsmen specially hired to come to al-Andalus to help beautify the mosque.

Later mosques followed in this tradition. For example, the markets were usually close to mosques, and village and town councils met in mosques. In a Muslim city, the ruler's or governor's palace was often next door to the Friday mosque. Rulers were recognized as legitimate by having their names mentioned in the Friday sermon. Authors published their books by having them read aloud in the mosque. Dinners for civic leaders might be held in a mosque's courtyard, and merchants might meet there to make business deals. Mosques also attracted vendors who sold such things as food, clothing, medicines, and books.

In the medieval Muslim world, especially in the cities, mosques played an important function as centers of law and learning. Many legal matters were judged according to religious law, based on the Qur'an and Sunna. Judges who heard cases on such matters generally held court at the mosque. Legal scholars might also teach in

The Mosque

mosques, as did scholars in other fields of religious studies. The teacher typically sat against a wall or column in the prayer hall, and the students sat in a semicircle around him (or, occasionally, her). From the 1100s on, many mosques were built with four covered porches, called *iwans*, around a rectangular courtyard. The largest *iwan* was the prayer hall, and the others could be used by judges and teachers.

This four-*iwan* design was also frequently employed in madrasas, which were the colleges or universities of the medieval Muslim world. Most of these schools were part of mosque complexes or were located nearby. Madrasas offered advanced instruction in the Qur'an, hadiths, and law, often with additional subjects such as literature, astronomy, and medicine. A few early madrasas have survived to the present, most notably the one founded at Cairo's al-Azhar Mosque in 972; it is Egypt's oldest university.

The teachers and students of madrasas were usually supported by charitable endowments called *waqfs*. A *waqf* was the income from property donated by a ruler or other wealthy person. *Waqfs* could fund the building and staffing not only of schools but also of soup kitchens,

Faith

travelers' shelters, and hospitals. These and similar institutions were often part of mosque complexes.

The widespread building of hospitals in particular has been called one of the medieval Muslim world's greatest achievements. These hospitals were far in advance of anything that could be found in Christian Europe at the time. They had separate sections for men and women. Many had specific units for surgical cases, contagious diseases, and other needs. Most hospitals were located in cities, but they often sent teams of doctors out to help people in rural villages.

Hospitals frequently gave their staff members on-site lodging and meals. Many hospitals had large medical libraries and offered training for student doctors. Moreover, medical care in medieval Muslim hospitals was available to everyone—whatever their age, gender, religion, or social class—free of charge. "Those who hoard gold and silver and do not spend it in the path of the Lord, tell them about a painful punishment," said the Qur'an. *Waqf* donors who supported hospitals could be certain that they were indeed spending their gold and silver in the path of God.

The courtyard and two *iwans* of Cairo's Mosque and Madrasa of Sultan Hassan, built in the 1350s. The madrasa's teachers held classes in the *iwans*, and students lived in rooms behind them. The *iwan* on the left faces Mecca, so has a *mihrab* at its center. The structure in front of the *mihrab* and *minbar* was used as a platform for Qur'an readers. In the middle of the courtyard is a covered fountain for washing before prayer.

The Mosque

THE EXCELLENCE OF KNOWLEDGE

One of the foremost medieval madrasas was the Nizamiyya, founded in Baghdad in 1067 by Nizam al-Mulk, who was the sultan Malik-Shah's vizier (chief administrator). The Nizamiyya numbered many prominent and gifted men among its students and teachers. The most renowned of them all was the Persian judge, scholar, and Sufi al-Ghazali (1058–1111), author of more than seventy books. His *Revival of Religious Sciences* has been one of the most influential works on Muslim spirituality for centuries.

Above: A teacher reads to his students, who are expected to commit their lessons to memory.

Al-Ghazali was noted for bringing together the scholarly and mystical approaches to Islam. Also, after making a thorough study of ancient Greek philosophy, al-Ghazali concluded that reason could not reveal spiritual truths—for this, faith was required. Nevertheless, al-Ghazali did not reject learning but embraced the pursuit of knowledge, which he praised in the first section of *Revival of Religious Sciences*:

In tradition, the Prophet . . . said, "Whoever follows a path in search of knowledge, [God] will guide him into a path leading into Paradise." And again, "Verily the angels will bow low to the seeker after knowledge in approval of what he does." He also said, "To rise up before daybreak and learn but a section of knowledge is better than prostrating yourself in prayer a hundred times." . . . And again, "Seeking after knowledge is an ordinance obligatory upon every Muslim." . . .

The greatest achievement in the opinion of man is eternal happiness and the most excellent thing is the way which leads to it. This happiness will never be attained except through knowledge and works, and works are impossible without the knowledge of how they are done. The basis for happiness in this world and the next is knowledge. Of all works it is, therefore, the most excellent. And why not, since the excellence of anything is revealed by the quality of its fruit. You have already learnt that the fruit of knowledge in the hereafter is drawing near to the Lord of the Universe, attaining the rank of the angels, and joining the company of the heavenly hosts. Its fruits in this world, however, are power, dignity, influence over kings, and reverence from all. . . .

The excellences of teaching and learning . . . are therefore manifest [obvious]. For if knowledge is the most excellent of things, the process of acquiring it would then be a search for the most excellent, and imparting it would be promoting the most excellent. For human interests extend to both the material and the spiritual worlds, and no order exists in the latter without existing in the former because this world is a preparation for the next, and is the instrument which leads to [God] anyone who uses it as such, a home for him who takes it as a dwelling place.

After Prayers at the Mosque, a painting by Rudolph Ernst, who visited Morocco, Egypt, and Turkey in the late 1800s. In his paintings he combined designs, clothing, and objects from all these countries, rather than portraying specific people and places.

Men of Piety and Learning

Verily, the men of knowledge are the inheritors of the prophets.
→ A SAYING OF MUHAMMAD

UHAMMAD HAD BEEN THE *UMMA'S* SPIRITUAL and political leader. His first four successors (known as the *rashidun*, or "rightly guided" caliphs) fulfilled the same dual role. But the Muslim world quickly became too large and diverse for one man to decide on every matter that affected life and worship for everyone in every part of the Dar al-Islam. Moreover, as the caliphs strived to hold all this territory together, they gradually became more like traditional kings, absolute monarchs whose lives were very different from those of average Muslims. Then, in the tenth century, the caliphs began to lose political power. Actual government was handled by viziers (chief administrators), emirs (governors and military commanders), and sultans. Still, the caliph remained an important symbol of the *umma*'s unity until 1258, when Mongol invaders destroyed Baghdad and killed the caliph.

COMMUNITY LEADERS

As the caliphs became more distant and symbolic figures, people looked closer to home for religious guidance and leadership. Islam had no priests, because no one could stand between the believer and God—"We shall not erect, from among ourselves, lords and patrons other than God," said the Qur'an. A Muslim's relationship with God was his or her own personal responsibility, and every Muslim had equal access to God's blessings. There were men, however, who distinguished themselves by their superior learning and, ideally, righteous living.

These religious scholars, the *ulama* ("men with knowledge"), worked hard to define the "straight path" that Muslims should follow. They had endless discussions and many disagreements—but that was acceptable. Muhammad had said, "The difference of view among the scholars of my community is a blessing from God." There was strength in diversity: considering a variety of opinions and interpretations could often lead to new and stronger understanding of what it meant to submit to God's will.

The *ulama* were particularly concerned with making sure that the laws guiding society were in harmony with Islam. Although the government was expected to uphold the laws, it was the *ulama* who defined and interpreted them. There were four main schools of Sunni legal theory, but in general the *ulama* agreed on basic principles. For example, anything a Muslim did fell into one of five categories of action: required, recommended, permitted, not recommended, or forbidden. These categories gave people ethical as well as legal guidelines. Similarly, every Muslim had two basic sets of obligations: duties to

God (the Five Pillars) and duties to others. Such concerns as crime and punishment, contracts, and family law all related to people's duty to others.

The most important source of Islamic law, called Sharia, was the Qur'an. When it did not give enough guidance on a particular subject, the next place to look was the hadiths. If the matter was still unclear, scholars turned to *ijma*, the accepted customs of the community, since Muhammad had said, "My community will never agree on an error." *Ijma* could also refer more specifically to the principles that the majority of judges and legal theorists had agreed on.

A page from an Andalusian Qur'an. The text comes from the fourth chapter, the source of much of Islamic law concerning women and marriage.

One other source of law was *ijtihad* ("mental striving"), the scholar's independent reasoning. However, by the eleventh century most Sunni *ulama* believed that the "gate of *ijtihad*" was closed—the time when individual interpretations of the law were acceptable had passed.* Nevertheless, judges had some flexibility in applying the law, which in many areas was regarded as more of an ideal than something that could be strictly enforced.

The *ulama* were mainly teachers, judges, lawyers, and legal consultants. Other religious officials who played important roles in worship and community life included the muezzins, who chanted the call to prayer. In the mosque an imam, or leader, stood at the front of the prayer hall and led the rest of the congregation in *salat*. A man called a *muqri* recited or read from the Qur'an. On Fridays a *khatib*, or preacher,

---

*Shi'i Muslims had their own schools of legal theory and their own collections of hadiths. The Shi'i schools generally did not accept *ijma* as a source of law, but did accept the continuing use of *ijtihad*.

Nineteenth-century British artist John Frederick Lewis, who lived in Cairo for nine years, captured the patience of the teacher and the different moods of the children (and animals) in this lively classroom scene.

gave the official sermon. Some of these men earned only part of their living at the mosque and might also work at a trade or in business.

A full-time occupation was that of *muhtasib*. This word is usually translated as "market inspector," but that was only part of his job. In the market, it was his duty (aided by his assistants) to maintain order and honesty. He made sure that the marketplace and the streets leading to it were kept clean and clear, he put a stop to fights and disorderly conduct, and he made sure that merchants sold quality goods and did not cheat their customers. His broader task, though, was "to promote what is right and prevent what is wrong." This duty was called *hisba*, which the scholar and Sufi al-Ghazali called "the main pivot of the religion, and the high purpose for which God sent His Prophets."

According to al-Ghazali and others, every Muslim was required to practice *hisba*. The *muhtasib*, however, was a *hisba* specialist, and he was expected to stop any dangerous or immoral behavior that occurred in public. He was not allowed to invade people's privacy, though, and he had to catch them in the act. The *muhtasib* dealt with a range of offenses, which could include refusal to fast during Ramadan, public drunkenness, cruelty to animals, theft, and even more serious matters. Ideally the *muhtasib* would be able to stop the problem with just his powers of persuasion. If that didn't work, he would scold and then, if necessary, threaten the offender. Next the *muhtasib* would try to physically restrain the offender, but he would use force and weapons only as a last resort.

MYSTICS AND POETS

The original, literal meaning of *Sharia* was "the road to the watering hole"—the route to water, the source and sustainer of life. It is easy to see how this word came to refer to the divinely guided path to the Creator. Law and ethics were not the only way to God, though. For many men, Sufi mysticism was a more direct and fulfilling path. It was also a difficult one, requiring sacrifices and intense discipline. For instance, to avoid being distracted by worldly concerns, Sufis often decided not to marry or have children—a choice frowned on by society, especially the *ulama*. Like some groups of Christian and Buddhist monks in the Middle Ages, many Sufis also chose to live in poverty, and might earn their only living by begging.*

Sufis dedicated many years to study, meditation, and other spiritual practices. A person who wanted to follow this path would find a Sufi master, or *shaykh*, and become his pupil or disciple. Some student Sufis studied with a number of masters (occasionally women as well as men), and might travel great distances to do so. The *shaykhs* taught various techniques of purifying the soul, reaching spiritual ecstasy, and understanding the mystical meanings of the Qur'an and hadiths.

Dervish, the Persian word for a Muslim mystic, literally meant "beggar."

Men of Piety and Learning

Sufis dance to the accompaniment of flute and tambourines. An elderly Sufi, who has collapsed in the ecstasy of losing "all consciousness of this world," is tended by a young disciple.

Starting in the eleventh century, many Sufi *shaykhs* ran centers called *khanaqas*. A *khanaqa* was similar to a madrasa, and the building usually included a prayer hall, a kitchen, and a number of small, plain bedrooms. It was a place where devout people could stay for a while to study with the *shaykh* or simply to spend time in prayer and other religious observances.*

One of the main forms of Sufi devotional practice was the *dhikr*, "remembrance," in which Sufis made themselves mindful of God, often by chanting God's titles—the Merciful, the Compassionate, the Beautiful, the Truth, and so on. Many Sufis also used music, dance, and poetry as forms of worship. Al-Ghazali wrote one of the earliest descriptions of these practices and their effects in his book *The Alchemy of Happiness*:

> By means of music, [the Sufis] often obtain spiritual visions and ecstasies, their hearts becoming in this condition as clean as silver in the flame of a furnace, and attaining a degree of purity which could never be attained by any amount of mere outward austerities. The Sufi then becomes so keenly aware of his relationship to the spiritual world that he loses all consciousness of this world. . . .

*Most *khanaqas* were for men only, but there were a small number for just women.

Faith

Although Sufis generally tried to live humble lives, seeking neither wealth nor fame, a number of them became well known for their teachings and writings. Many expressed their ideas in poetry. The Andalusian mystic Ibn al-Arabi (1165–1240) expanded on the idea of the oneness of God so central to Islamic belief. He based his conception of the Creator on a famous hadith in which God said, "I was a hidden treasure and wanted to be known, thus I created the world that I might be known." Ibn al-Arabi wrote many poems expressing his belief that God's oneness pervaded all creation. He often used bold language to communicate this "unity of being" and the close relationship he sought to have with God. For example:

> He knows me, while I know naught of Him,
> I also know Him and perceive Him.
> Where then is His self-sufficiency,
> Since I help Him and grant Him Bliss?
> It is for this that the Reality created me,
> For I give content to His Knowledge and manifest Him.

In other words, Ibn al-Arabi, like everything else in the world, was created so that God could be perceived by the senses—because everything God made was part of him. In this way God could know himself, and through his creation humans could in turn know him. Many people felt that such ideas were not in keeping with true Islam, and Ibn al-Arabi's works were banned in some parts of the Islamic world for hundreds of years. But numerous other Muslims regarded Ibn al-Arabi as the greatest of all Sufi masters, and his concept of the unity of being was embraced by most of the Muslim mystics who came after him.

A portrait of Rumi from the religious center he founded in Konya, where numerous pilgrims come every year to visit his tomb

RUMI

Among Westerners today, the most renowned of all Sufis is Jalal ad-Din ar-Rumi (1207–1273). Rumi was born in Persian-speaking Afghanistan but settled in Konya in Anatolia, where he became the founder of the Mevlevi Sufi order, sometimes called the Whirling Dervishes. Since Rumi's time, the Mevlevi have used a slow, dancelike, spinning movement to bring about a state in which they are temporarily freed from personal limits so that they can experience spiritual ecstasy, a sense of the divine unity of being.

Rumi was also a poet, whose works sought to convey the sense of rapture that he experienced in whirling and his other devotions to God. To produce this effect, he used words and phrases that might seem contradictory, images of love or drunkenness, and other unusual comparisons and ideas. Here is a selection:

What can I do, Muslims? I do not know myself.

I am neither Christian nor Jew, neither Magian nor Muslim,

I am not from east or west, not from land or sea. . . .

My place is placeless, my trace is traceless,

no body, no soul, I am from the soul of souls.

I have chased out duality, lived the two worlds as one.

One I seek, one I know, one I see, one I call.

He is the first, he is the last, he is the outer, he is the inner.

Beyond "He" and "He is" I know no other.

I am drunk from the cup of love, the two worlds have escaped me.

I have no concern but carouse and rapture.

If one day in my life I spend a moment without you

from that hour and that time I would repent my life.

If one day I am given a moment in solitude with you

I will trample the two worlds underfoot and dance forever. . . .

For centuries camel litters were a convenient mode of transport for women in Arabia and Syria. They were still a common way to travel in the 1800s, when this illustration was made

SIX

Women in Islam

Be intimately conscious of God as regards women, and strive to be good to them.

➤➤ MUHAMMAD'S FAREWELL SERMON

OVER THE CENTURIES, THERE HAVE BEEN NUMEROUS controversies about women's rights and roles in the Muslim world. The Qur'an's statements about women have sometimes been given widely differing meanings. One verse, for example, has been interpreted to mean, "Men have authority over women because God has made the one superior to the other." But here is another interpretation of the very same verse:

> (Husbands) are the protectors
> And maintainers of their (wives)
> Because God has given
> The one more (strength)

Than the other, and because
They support them
From their means.

One interpretation makes the verse a statement about male superiority, while the other makes it a statement about husbands' responsibilities to their wives. Which view is closest to the Qur'an's intention? The people of the medieval Muslim world answered questions like this in a variety of ways, and the answers had a range of effects on women's lives.

MUHAMMAD'S REFORMS

In much of pre-Islamic Arabia, men were in charge of just about everything, and their power was almost unlimited. A woman was basically the property of her father until marriage, and she could be married, without her consent, to anyone her father chose. She then became the property of her husband and had no right to divorce, even if he abused her or failed to support her. The husband could marry as many other wives as he wanted. When he died, his male heirs inherited his wives along with the rest of his property. Women, on the other hand, could not inherit anything.

Arabia was a land of scarcity. Crops could be grown only in scattered oases, and much of the peninsula's population was nomadic, traveling with their livestock from place to place in search of water and fresh pastures on the desert fringes. Competition for resources was intense, and tribes made much of their living by raiding other tribes. Women rarely (if ever) participated in the raids, so it was felt that they contributed little to the tribe's livelihood. For this and other reasons, sons were much more highly valued than daughters. When a baby girl was born, the father might decide not to raise her, espe-

cially if times were hard, and she would be buried alive in the desert.

Muhammad's revelations told him that all of this was wrong. Over and over, the Qur'an stated that women's submission to God was equal to that of men, that both had the same religious duties and the same heavenly rewards; for instance: "Those who surrender themselves to God and accept the true Faith; who are devout, sincere, patient, humble, charitable and chaste; who fast and are ever mindful of God—on these, both men and women, God will bestow forgiveness and a rich reward." Under Islam, women could no longer be treated as property—as Muhammad said, according to a hadith, "Women are but sisters (shaqa'iq, or twin halves) of men."

Islam gave women full rights to own property and make contracts (rights that women in many Christian countries would not have for centuries). Inheritance rights, too, were guaranteed: "From what is left by parents and those nearest related, there is a share for men and a

Women in nomadic tribes did not live in seclusion from men the way wealthy city women often did. Nevertheless, it was generally considered proper for a woman to cover her face in the presence of a male visitor from outside the family.

Women in Islam

share for women, whether the property be large or small," said the Qur'an, and specified the percentages that sons and daughters should receive. Daughters did, however, inherit a smaller portion—it was assumed that they would be supported by their husbands, while sons would have wives and children they must provide for.

As for daughters, the Qur'an absolutely condemned the killing of baby girls—it was one of the crimes that people would have to answer for on Judgment Day. The Qur'an also made it clear that it was wrong for parents to be upset by the birth of a girl instead of a boy. And the Prophet said, "Whosoever has a daughter and does not bury her alive, does not insult her, and does not favor his son over her, [God] will enter him into Paradise." He set the example by the way he treated his own daughters, especially his youngest, Fatima, who was his lifelong student and supporter.

MARRIAGE AND MODESTY

"Marriage," said Muhammad, "is one half of religion." Nearly everyone in the medieval Muslim world, male and female, expected to marry. Most marriages were arranged by the families, but Muhammad established the woman's right to reject a match. A hadith told how a young woman came to Muhammad because her father had made her marry without even asking her opinion. Because she had not given her consent, Muhammad said he would dissolve the marriage for her. She replied, "Actually, I accept this marriage, but I wanted to let women know that parents have no right to force a husband on them."

In pre-Islamic Arabia, the husband paid a dowry (money, goods, livestock, or other property) to his bride's father, but the Qur'an changed this, telling men, "Give women their dowry as a free gift." The dowry was the wife's property for the rest of her life, to do with as she wished. Her husband had no right to it—to take it from her "would be improper and grossly unjust," even if the marriage ended. Women also gained the right to seek divorce, and to receive child support from their children's father (rights that were not available to most women in Christian Europe until modern times).

Divorce was considered the last resort if a marriage was not going well. Before taking this step, the couple should turn to mediators to help them work things out. If the problem was that the husband didn't like something about his wife's behavior, there were recommended steps he could take, including reasoning with her or sleeping apart from her for a time. The Qur'an also strongly advised that he try to see her point of view and focus on her positive traits. If, however, the wife responded with contempt, he was permitted to lightly slap her. Beating a wife was never acceptable to Muhammad—he told the men of the *umma*, "Only the worst of you will have recourse to such methods."

The Qur'an instructed husbands to live with their wives "on a footing of kindness and equity." It limited the number of wives a man could have to four, and only if he could treat them all equally. The ideal, though, was to have just one wife, for both emotional and financial reasons, and this was the most common situation. Few

Women and children leave their village mosque together on the night of the Prophet's birthday. It has been common for women in the Muslim world to hold their own gatherings and celebrations, separate from men's.

men could afford to support four wives and their children. Moreover, most women preferred to be the only wife, and they could make this a condition of their marriage contracts. Nevertheless, marrying two or more women could be valuable to society. The most important reason to do so was to make sure that widows and their children were provided for.

Muhammad demonstrated both approaches to marriage in his own life. He never took another wife for as long as Khadija was alive. In Medina, though, he eventually had eleven wives—more than the number allowed other Muslims because of his responsibilities as leader of the community. Most of these women were widows, some of whose husbands had been killed during the *umma*'s battles for survival. And many of the marriages helped Muhammad strengthen his and the *umma*'s ties with important allies. Each wife had her own little house next to the mosque's courtyard, and Muhammad was careful to stay with each wife for an equal amount of time.

Unfortunately, the houses' nearness to the mosque, with the constant comings and goings there, gave Muhammad and his family little privacy. Many people also pestered Muhammad's wives to ask him for favors and that sort of thing. Moreover, on a few occasions his enemies tried to hurt him by accusing one of his wives of improper behavior. Responding to these problems, the Qur'an said, "Oh you who have attained the faith! Do not enter the Prophet's dwellings unless you are given leave. . . . And as for the Prophet's wives, whenever you ask them for anything that you need, ask them from behind a screen."

Additional verses revealed around the same time said, "Wives of the Prophet, you are not like other women. . . . Stay in your homes and do not display your finery as women used to do in the days of ignorance." In Islam's second century, the *ulama* began to apply

Faith

these verses to all Muslim women. More and more, respectable women were expected to live in seclusion in their homes. And although the Qur'an told both men and women to "lower their gaze and guard their modesty," in many places women (but not men) were required to veil their faces in public.

Other cultures the Muslims came into contact with played a large role in spreading such practices—for example, upper-class Byzantine women had been living in private women's quarters and wearing veils for centuries. In many ways, local customs and old habits often had a stronger influence on women's lives than did the teachings of Islam. Numerous medieval Muslim women, especially in rural areas where

The harem, or women's quarters, of a wealthy Muslim home, as imagined by British artist John Frederick Lewis.

there were few opportunities for education, probably did not even know what their legal and religious rights were. Muhammad had made great efforts to improve the lives and status of women. Nevertheless, as in the rest of the ancient and medieval world, most men still treated them as though they were inferior.

LEADERS AND TEACHERS

During Muhammad's lifetime and for many decades afterward, women were able to play a variety of public roles in the *umma*. Muhammad valued the opinions of his wives and his female Companions, making it a practice to discuss religious and community matters with them. When he went on journeys and military campaigns, he almost always took one of his wives along. A number of women participated in warfare in different ways. Most commonly they carried water and nursed the wounded, something that Muhammad's daughter Fatima in particular was known for. Occasionally they picked up swords and fought alongside the men, like the Medinan woman Nusaybah bint Kab during one of the early *umma*'s fiercest battles with Mecca.

In chapter 3 we saw how Muhammad's widow Aisha led the uprising against the caliph Ali. After her defeat at the Battle of the Camel (called that because much of the fighting took place around the camel she was riding), she retired to her house in Medina. There she became a great religious teacher, passing on some two thousand hadiths. They ranged from spiritually profound statements to touching pictures of Muhammad's everyday life—for example, when he wasn't needed at the mosque, he did household chores, "sewed his clothes, [and] repaired his shoes." Throughout the Middle Ages, many women followed in Aisha's footsteps as notable hadith teachers and religious scholars.

Faith

"No god but God," carved into marble in the eleventh century

THE OPENING

The first chapter of the Qur'an is called al-Fatiha, "The Opening." Since the time of Muhammad it has been recited in all formal prayers, and its first line begins almost every chapter of the Qur'an. This line had added meaning for women and may have helped influence them to embrace Islam in its early years. In Arabic, the divine names translated as "the Compassionate" and "the Merciful" are feminine nouns and are closely related to words having to do with pregnancy and motherhood. This is one of many examples of the ways the Qur'an used language that spoke equally to women and men. Here is The Opening:

In the name of God, the Merciful and Compassionate. Praise be to God, Lord of the Universe, the Merciful and Compassionate. Ruler on the Day of Judgment. You do we worship and call upon for help. Guide us along the Straight Path, the road of those whom You have favored, those with whom You are not angry, who are not lost.

Some *ulama*, though, blamed Aisha for her part in the Battle of the Camel, for becoming involved in the politics that divided the *umma*. The *ulama* used this as a reason to claim that women would cause harm if they tried to play a role in public life, particularly a leadership role. This was most people's opinion in the Middle Ages (in Christian Europe as well as in the Muslim world), even though there was no basis for it in the Qur'an or hadiths. In fact in the Qur'an, Bilqis, the queen of Sheba, was an honored figure. And occasionally parts of the medieval Muslim world were ruled by women, such as the Shi'i queen Arwa, who governed Yemen from 1067 to 1138.

Women could and did lead at lower levels of society, too. Some early scholars said it was possible for qualified women to serve as judges in Sharia courts. We know that the second caliph appointed a woman as *muhtasib* in Medina. In fact, the only religious role that was really closed to a woman was leading men in prayer, because she would be in front of them and her prostrations would place her in an immodest position. But even here an exception could be made, as the legal theorist Ibn Taymiyah (1263–1328) wrote: "It is permissible for an illiterate man to be led in prayers by a woman who is a reciter of the Qur'an . . . in Ramadan, according to the . . . opinion of Ahmad (Ibn Hanbal*)." This also shows that women could be Qur'an reciters. And they could lead other women in prayer without any problem.

In the early decades of Islam, women routinely went to the mosque to pray. Because of the postures of prayer, they lined up behind the men. Later, women had their own section in some mosques, often separated from the men by a screen or other par-

*Ahmad ibn Hanbal (780–855) was the founder of one of the four major Sunni schools of legal theory.

tition. But in many areas, women were gradually discouraged from going to the mosque at all and were expected to pray in the same way they did almost everything else, in the privacy of the home. Here, it was felt, was where their primary duty lay: to run the household and bring up children in the faith.

Nevertheless, there were still ways in which some women, at least, could play public or semipublic roles in religious life. Wealthy women were often *waqf* donors, funding the building and maintenance of mosques, madrasas, and other institutions. In addition to the women scholars, or *awalim*, there were also many women Sufis. Like the *awalim*, they frequently taught men as well as women; a female Sufi master was called a *shaykha*. Some women taught in their homes, but others were able to teach (and study) in mosques, schools, or *khanaqas*.

One of the earliest and most famous women Sufis was Rabia al-Adawiyya (died in 801), who lived in Basra, Iraq. Completely devoted to God, she never married. She was renowned for her holiness and her teachings about the love of God. Rabia also wrote beautiful and moving religious poetry, such as this verse:

O my Lord, if I worship you from fear of Hell
burn me in Hell.
If I worship you from hope of Paradise,
exclude me from that place.
But if I worship you for your own sake,
do not withhold from me your eternal beauty.

Above: Muhammad with his daughter Fatima (in red), his wives Aisha and Umm Salama, and other women of his household. Fatima became especially revered by Shi'i Muslims, while Aisha was the woman most honored by Sunnis. Celebrated for her learning, Aisha was also a role model for women who pursued religious studies.

A Shaykha

One of the Sufi masters who taught Ibn al-Arabi in Seville was a woman named Nuna
Fatima. He wrote that when he began studying with her, "she was already more than ninety
years old. She ate extremely little, living on scraps of left-over food that people threw in
front of their door. However . . . one might have taken her for a fourteen-year-old girl, so
lovely and tender was she to look on." Nuna Fatima had other remarkable qualities, which
Ibn al-Arabi described in a story about the power of her faith. One day a woman came to
her for help: her husband had taken a wife in another town, and the woman wanted him
to come back. Nuna Fatima declared she would send the Fatiha (the opening sura, or chapter, of the Qur'an) to the man to summon him home. Then, wrote Ibn al-Arabi,

> I recognized her spiritual power, for as she recited the *sura*, it gradually
> assumed a physical, albeit ethereal form. Once she had formed it, I heard
> her say to it, "O *Fatiha*, go . . . and fetch this woman's husband. Do not
> leave him alone, until he comes with you." The time it would take to cover
> this distance had not yet elapsed when the man arrived. Immediately, my
> mentor took up a tambourine in her hand and began to strike it as a sign
> of rejoicing. I asked her why she was doing this, and she said to me, "By
> God, I am really happy that He takes notice of me; for He has made me one
> of His trusted friends and drawn me to Him. And who am I, that this Lord
> should have singled me out . . . ? By the glory of my Lord and Master, I
> swear that He keeps such a close watch over my love, that I myself am
> unable to measure it."

SEVEN

Holy Days and Every Day

Behold, my prayer, and [all] my acts of worship and my living and my dying
are for God [alone], the Sustainer of all the worlds.

→→ QUR'AN 6:162

SLAM MEANS "SUBMISSION," IN THE SENSE OF choosing God's will over human wants and of giving oneself wholeheartedly to God. The word is also related to Arabic *salam*, "peace." The first thing the angel Gabriel said to Muhammad was *As-salam alaykum* ("Peace be upon you"), and Muslims have greeted one another with these words throughout the *umma*'s existence. Another everyday phrase that Muslims have used since the time of the Prophet is *in sha Allah* (often spelled *inshallah*), "if God so wills" or "God willing." The practice of saying this when making plans came from a verse of the Qur'an: "Never say of anything, 'I shall do that tomorrow,' except: 'If God so wills,' and remember

Opposite: The *mihrab* showed the way to Mecca in this world and to heaven in the next.

77

your Lord when you forget, and say: 'I hope that my Lord will guide me ever closer than this to the right course.'"

These phrases are only two examples of the ways Islam became woven into the fabric of everyday life. We have read about many others, too, from legal principles to cleanliness to the ways men and women dressed. Islam also played a role in what people ate and drank. Intoxicating substances were forbidden by the Qur'an, and the *ulama* generally agreed that all alcoholic beverages were off-limits. Muslims also could not eat pork or any meat from an animal that had not been properly slaughtered. Muhammad had cared about the well-being of all living things, and once said, "Whoever kills a sparrow or a bigger animal without respecting its right to exist will be accountable to God for it on the Day of Judgment." Therefore, killing an animal for food should be done prayerfully and quickly, causing the animal as little fear and pain as possible.

DAYS OF PRAYER AND PRAISE

Five times a day, every day, the call to prayer rang out in every city, town, and village of the Dar al-Islam, beginning with the words *Allahu Akbar*—"God is greater!"—proclaimed four times. It was a reminder that whatever the Muslim was doing, God was more important. It was time to stop work, wherever you were, and pray. If someone was engaged in a task that really couldn't be interrupted— for example, a midwife delivering a baby—this was still an opportunity to be mindful of God, and the missed prayers could be performed later in the day.

For the noon prayer on Friday, Muslims (or at least all the adult men in the community) were expected to assemble at the mosque, unless they were physically unable to get there. The Qur'an instructed, "Believers, when you are summoned to Friday prayers,

hasten to the remembrance of God and cease your trading. That would be best for you, if you but knew it. Then when the prayers are ended, disperse and go your ways in quest of God's bounty." During the Middle Ages, Fridays were not, as they are now, a day of rest when all business ceased, but they were still special days. Before the noon prayer, many Muslims bathed and put on perfume and their best clothes, then enjoyed a family meal after the service.

Standing, sitting, or kneeling on mats and prayer rugs, men move through the different stages of prayer in the mosque. An Italian artist painted this scene in 1884.

During the month of Ramadan there were special prayers and routines, including the recitation of the entire Qur'an, one portion each day. Muslims got up very early so that they could eat breakfast before sunrise. Those who were fasting (ideally, all healthy adults) would not eat or drink again till after the evening prayer. Throughout the day they were also supposed to be extra careful not to lie, speak harshly, or have negative thoughts. These spiritual disciplines would purify Muslims and bring them closer to God. After dark they would enjoy the closeness of family and friends at meals

Holy Days and Every Day

that often featured sweets and other foods eaten only during the nights of Ramadan. The first thing served at these dinners tradition- ally was a dish of dates, as this was how Muhammad was said to have ended his fasts.

The end of Ramadan was a great holiday, Eid al-Fitr, the Feast of the Breaking of the Fast. Celebrations might last for three days. People enjoyed delicious foods. Often they had new clothes for the occasion, and they might visit friends and relatives and exchange gifts. It was also a time to give food and money to the poor. In many cities there were splendid processions, in which government officials and military officers paraded in gorgeous robes to the accompaniment of trumpets and kettledrums. Another major holiday, with similar cele- brations, was Eid al-Adha, the Feast of Sacrifice. As we saw in chapter 2, through this feast all Muslims, wherever they were, were connected to the climax of the annual pilgrimage to Mecca.

Many people observed the birthday of the Prophet (Mawlid al- Nabi) as a holiday. Sunni Muslims did not adopt this custom until the late eleventh century, but it had become popular among Shi'is at least a century earlier. Shi'is also commemorated events in the lives of Muhammad's family members, especially Ali and his son Husayn. The festival of Ghadir Khumm, for example, marked the occasion when, Shi'is believed, Muhammad chose Ali to be his suc- cessor. The most important Shi'i holy day, Ashura, occurred about three weeks later, on the tenth day of the first month of the year. On Ashura, Shi'is publicly mourned the death of Husayn. If they could, they made a pilgrimage to his tomb at Karbala, Iraq.

Husayn was not the only Shi'i Imam buried in Iraq: Ali's tomb was in Kufa, and there were others in Samarra and Baghdad. The Imams' burial sites were holy places to Shi'is, who visited them to weep for the sufferings of the Imams. Sincere weeping could help

Trumpeters and drummers lead a caravan on its way to Mecca for the annual pilgrimage. This is a modern copy of an illustration from a thirteenth-century Arabic manuscript.

earn the believer forgiveness of sins. According to one thirteenth-century Shi'i scholar, pilgrims to the Imams' tombs expressed their feelings this way: "Since the Lord of the future life takes pleasure in sorrow and since it serves to purify God's servants—behold! we therefore don mourning attire and find delight in letting tears flow. We say to the eyes: stream in uninterrupted weeping forever!"

By the 1100s Sunni Muslims, too, were making pilgrimages to the graves of holy people. They visited not only Muhammad's tomb in Medina and Fatima's in the same city, but also the burial places of revered scholars and Sufi masters, and the places where Abraham, Moses, David, Jesus, and other prophets had lived and died. Such people had been "friends of God," specially blessed, and the pilgrims hoped that at least a little of that blessing would rub off on them.

Holy Days and Every Day

STRUGGLE

When the Shi'i Buyid Dynasty ruled in Iraq, Baghdad's Sunni population sometimes held its own festivals to rival the Shi'i holidays. Sometimes, though, Sunnis responded to the Shi'is' public celebrations with violence. In 1055 the Sunni Seljuk Dynasty conquered Iraq, and Shi'is lost all political power there. In 1171 Egypt, too, returned to Sunni rule. But clashes between Shi'is and Sunnis would continue, off and on, all the way into modern times.

Muhammad had wanted his community to be one of peace, one where all Muslims were brothers and sisters, where Muslims never fought against Muslims. This was not to be. Few human communities have ever been able to avoid conflict, and the *umma* was no different. There were civil wars. There were rival dynasties. There were rival forces within dynasties. There were always people who craved power and were willing to use violence to get it. There were always troublemakers.

Most of the time, though, believers on different spiritual paths lived and worked together without problems. They recognized that, after all, many details of faith and religious law were simply matters of opinion. As al-Ghazali explained, "The heretic believes that he is right, and believes that the man of right belief is wrong; each claims that he is right, and denies that he is a heretic." Muslim authorities generally felt that social peace was a greater good than trying to force everyone to believe and worship in only one way.

This attitude usually extended to Jews, Christians, and followers of other religions as well. But there were times when violence broke out, especially between Muslims and Christians. There were raids, battles, invasions, and wars. People on both sides wanted land or booty or secure borders or any combination of the things that soldiers and their leaders have hoped to gain throughout history.

Sometimes people just wanted to protect themselves—or their holy places, or their faith, or their way of life.

When Muslims fought in the cause of Islam, they referred to their actions as jihad. Outside the Muslim world, this term has often been translated as "holy war." Its actual meaning, though, is "effort," "exertion," or "struggle." War was a type of jihad, and sometimes it was justified: the Qur'an taught, "Permission [to fight] is given to those against whom war is being wrongfully waged." But even in such circumstances, Muhammad urged Muslims to follow certain rules, which his Companion Abu Bakr passed on: "Do not kill women, children, and old people. Do not commit treacherous actions. . . . Do not destroy palm trees, do not burn houses and [grain fields], do not cut down fruit trees, and do not kill livestock

Nineteenth-century pilgrims look toward Jerusalem, as generations before and since have done. The city's name means "dwelling of peace," voicing the hope of all three faiths that honor it as a holy place.

Holy Days and Every Day

except when you are compelled to eat them." Moreover, the Qur'an said, any battle or war should end as soon as the enemy asked for peace: "If they incline toward peace, do you [also, in the same way] incline toward peace, and trust in God, for He is the One that hears and knows [all things]."

A very important hadith related a conversation between Muhammad and one of his Companions when they returned to Medina after a battle with the Meccans. Muhammad said, "We are back from the lesser jihad to the greater jihad." The Companion asked what the greater jihad was, and Muhammad replied, "It is fighting the self." That is, the greater jihad was the effort to put aside selfish desires and live each day according to God's will. This was the jihad of daily life, the major challenge for every Muslim.

In the first year of the Hegira, Muhammad had put his trust in God for both himself and his community. As he neared the outskirts of Medina, he proclaimed: "Spread peace, feed the hungry, honor kinship ties, pray while people sleep, you shall enter paradise in peace." That was his vision of what it meant to live in constant remembrance of God—and the vision began and ended with peace.

Glossary

ablution the washing of one's body or part of it; Muslims wash in preparation for prayer

al-Andalus the part of the Iberian Peninsula (modern Spain and Portugal) ruled by Muslims; also called Andalusia

Arab an inhabitant of the Arabian Peninsula or someone whose ancestors came from there

Byzantine Empire the Greek-speaking, eastern half of the ancient Roman Empire, with its capital at Constantinople. Arabic speakers generally referred to it as Rum ("Rome").

caliph (Arabic *khalifa*) the political and spiritual leader of the Muslim community, ruling as Muhammad's successor and deputy

calligraphy literally, "beautiful writing." In the Muslim world calligraphy became a refined and esteemed art form, often using highly stylized letters.

dhimmi (from *dhimma*, "pact" or "contract") a non-Muslim living under Muslim rule who enjoyed protection and religious freedom (sometimes limited to a certain extent) in exchange for paying an annual tax

dynasty a series of rulers, usually related by family ties

Gospel the first four books of the New Testament of the Bible, which told of the life and teachings of Jesus

hadith a statement by or about Muhammad by someone who knew him, reporting his words and deeds. Hadiths were passed on word for word from one person to another, and eventually were gathered into authoritative collections.

imam a man who led the prayers at the mosque; in general, a religious leader or teacher. Shi'i Islam also taught that there were seven or twelve Imams, descendants of Muhammad, who were the rightful leaders of the Dar al-Islam in its first centuries.

madrasa (literally, "a place of study") a college, often attached to a mosque, for in-depth study of the Qur'an, hadiths, law, and other subjects, mostly focusing on religion

muhtasib a market inspector (sometimes called *sahib al-suq* or *señor del zoco* in al-Andalus), whose duties could include enforcing public morality and keeping the peace as well as making sure that marketplace business was conducted properly

pilgrimage a journey or visit to a sacred place

revelation something that is revealed by God to humans

salat formal prayer, performed five times a day according to a set pattern

Sharia Islamic law

Sunna Muhammad's actions and habits; in general, the way he lived his life, as related in the hadiths

Syria during the medieval period often used as the common name for the eastern Mediterranean region, including the modern countries of Jordan, Israel, Palestine, and Lebanon as well as Syria

Torah the first five books of the Bible; also known as the Books of Moses or Books of the Law

ulama (literally "men with knowledge" or "learned men") scholars who studied and taught the Qur'an, hadiths, and religious law

umma the community of Muslims

Zoroastrian (or Magian) a follower of an ancient Persian religion

For Further Reading

Barber, Nicola. *Everyday Life in the Ancient Arab and Islamic World.* North Mankato, MN: Smart Apple Media, 2006.

Doak, Robin. *Empire of the Islamic World.* New York: Facts on File, 2005.

George, Linda S. *The Golden Age of Islam.* New York: Benchmark Books, 1998.

Gordon, Matthew S. *Islam (World Religions).* Revised edition. New York:

Faith

Facts On File, 2001.

Murphy, Claire Rudolf, et al. *Daughters of the Desert: Stories of Remarkable Women from Christian, Jewish, and Muslim Traditions.* Woodstock, VT: Skylight Paths Publishing, 2003.

Nicolle, David. *Historical Atlas of the Islamic World.* New York: Checkmark Books, 2003.

Yuan, Margaret Speaker, ed. *At Issue: Women in Islam.* Detroit, MI: Greenhaven Press, 2005.

Online Information

Bartel, Nick. *Medieval Islamic Cultures.*
http://www.sfusd.k12.ca.us/schwww/sch618/Islam_New_Main.html

Foundation for Science Technology and Civilisation. *Muslim Heritage.*
http://www.muslimheritage.com

Islam: Empire of Faith.
http://www.pbs.org/empires/islam

Stone, Caroline. "The Muhtasib."
http://www.saudiaramcoworld.com/issue/197705/the.muhtasib.htm

Unity Productions Foundation. *Cities of Light: The Rise and Fall of Islamic Spain.*
http://www.islamicspain.tv/index.html

Selected Bibliography

Ali, Abdullah Yusuf. *The Meaning of the Holy Qur'an.* Tenth Edition. Beltsville, MD: Amana Publications, 1999.

Armstrong, Karen. *Islam: A Short History.* New York: Modern Library, 2000.

Armstrong, Karen. *Muhammad: A Prophet for Our Time.* New York: HarperCollins, 2006.

Badawi, Jamal. *Gender Equity in Islam: Basic Principles.* Burr Ridge, IL: American Trust Publications, 1995.

Burckhardt, Titus. *Moorish Culture in Spain.* Translated by Alisa Jaffa. New York: McGraw-Hill, 1972.

Esposito, John L. *Islam: The Straight Path.* 3rd edition. New York: Oxford University Press, 1998.

Irwin, Robert. *Islamic Art in Context: Art, Architecture, and the Literary World.* New York: Harry N. Abrams, 1997.

Lapidus, Ira M. *A History of Islamic Societies.* Cambridge: Cambridge University Press, 1988.

Lewis, Bernard, trans. *Music of a Distant Drum: Classical Arabic, Persian, Turkish, and Hebrew Poems.* Princeton, NJ: Princeton University Press, 2001.

Lindsay, James E. *Daily Life in the Medieval Islamic World.* Westport, CT: Greenwood Press, 2005.

Lowney, Chris. *A Vanished World: Muslims, Christians, and Jews in Medieval Spain.* New York: Oxford University Press, 2005.

McNeill, William H., and Marilyn Robinson Waldman, eds. *The Islamic World* (Readings in World History, vol. 6). New York: Oxford University Press, 1973.

Nasr, Seyyed Hossein. *Islam: Religion, History, and Civilization.* New York: HarperCollins, 2003.

O'Shea, Stephen. *Sea of Faith: Islam and Christianity in the Medieval Mediterranean World.* New York: Walker, 2006.

Faith

Ramadan, Tariq. *In the Footsteps of the Prophet: Lessons from the Life of Muhammad.* New York: Oxford University Press, 2007.

Robinson, Francis, ed. *The Cambridge Illustrated History of the Islamic World.* Cambridge: Cambridge University Press, 1996.

Sources for Quotations

Chapter 1

p. 13 "There is no god": Esposito, *Islam*, p. 68.

p. 16 "When it was the night": McNeill and Waldman, *The Islamic World*, pp. 20–21.

p. 16 "By the pen": Qur'an 68:1–3, in Ramadan, *In the Footsteps of the Prophet*, p. 31.

p. 17 "He is God": Qur'an 112, in Ramadan, *In the Footsteps of the Prophet*, p. 56.

Chapter 2

p. 21 "O believers": Esposito, *Islam*, p. 22.

p. 21 "it comes unto me": Armstrong, *Muhammad*, p. 57.

p. 21 "Never once": ibid., p. 56.

p. 23 "to free a slave": Qur'an 90:13-16, in Armstrong, *Muhammad*, p. 62.

p. 24 "There is no god": Qur'an 3:2-4, in Ramadan, *In the Footsteps of the Prophet*, p. 89.

p. 24 "You have indeed": Qur'an 33:21, in Ramadan, *In the Footsteps of the Prophet*, p. 43.

p. 24 "His character": Ramadan, *In the Footsteps of the Prophet*, p. x.

p. 25 "Yes, indeed" and "We have not sent": ibid., p. 64.

p. 25 "How fine and noble" and "I have come": Armstrong, *Muhammad*, p. 83.

p. 25 "When I heard": ibid., p. 84.

p. 26 "I am but a man": Qur'an 18:110, in Ramadan, *In the Footsteps of the Prophet*, p. x.

p. 26 "Islam has been built": Lindsay, *Daily Life in the Medieval Islamic World*, p. 139.

p. 27 Hadiths from Ramadan, *In the Footsteps of the Prophet*, pp. 102, 112–113, and 212; and Nasr, *Islam*, p. 56.

p. 28 "for the poor": Qur'an 9:60, in Lindsay, *Daily Life in the Medieval Islamic World*, p. 149.

p. 29 "If any one": Qur'an 2:184–185, in Lindsay, *Daily Life in the Medieval Islamic World*, p. 151.

p. 31 "And when they": Qur'an 37:103–109, in Lindsay, *Daily Life in the Medieval Islamic World*, p. 158.

Chapter 3

p. 33 "Know ye": Esposito, *Islam*, p. 11.

p. 35 "Do not argue": Qur'an 29:46, in Armstrong, *Islam*, p. 10.

p. 36 "There shall be": Qur'an 2:256, in Armstrong, *Islam*, p. 10.

p. 40 *ahl al-sunnah*: Nasr, *Islam*, p. 10.

p. 40 "enjoin good": Qur'an 9:112, in Ali, *The Meaning of the Holy Qur'an*, p. 471.

p. 41 "The lower (material) world": Esposito, *Islam*, p. 101.

p. 41 "*Ihsan* is": Nasr, *Islam*, p. 58.

p. 41 "Wheresoever ye turn": Qur'an 2:115, in Armstrong, *Islam*, p. 92.

Chapter 4

p. 43 "God builds": Irwin, *Islamic Art in Context*, p. 62.

p. 43 "The whole earth": Ramadan, *In the Footsteps of the Prophet*, p. 84.

p. 45 "God is the Light": Qur'an 24:35, in Irwin, *Islamic Art in Context*, p. 62.

p. 46 "When a believer": Ramadan, *In the Footsteps of the Prophet*, pp. 231–232.

p. 49 "Those who hoard": Qur'an 9:34, in Irwin, *Islamic Art in Context*, p. 83.

p. 51 "In tradition": *The Book of Knowledge*, online at

Faith

http://www.ghazali.org/works/bk1-sec-1.htm

Chapter 5

p. 53 "Verily, the men": Robinson, *Cambridge Illustrated History of the Islamic World*, p. 221.

p. 54 "We shall not erect": Qur'an 3:64, in Ramadan, *In the Footsteps of the Prophet*, p. 115.

p. 54 "The difference": Nasr, *Islam*, p. 9.

p. 55 "My community": Esposito, *Islam*, p. 82.

p. 56 "to promote": Robinson, *Cambridge Illustrated History of the Islamic World*, p. 175.

p. 56 "the main pivot": ibid., p. 176.

p. 57 "the road": Esposito, *Islam*, p. 78.

p. 58 "By means of music": "Concerning Music and Dancing as Aids to the Religious Life," online at http://en.wikisource.org/wiki/The_Alchemy_of_Happiness

p. 59 "I was a hidden": Robinson, *Cambridge Illustrated History of the Islamic World*, p. 235.

p. 59 "He knows me": Lowney, *A Vanished World*, p. 181.

p. 61 "What can I do": Lewis, *Music of a Distant Drum*, pp. 122–123.

Chapter 6

p. 63 "Be intimately conscious": Ramadan, *In the Footsteps of the Prophet*, p. 196.

p. 63 "Men have authority": Qur'an 4:34, in Lindsay, *Daily Life in the Medieval Islamic World*, p. 180.

p. 63 "(Husbands) are the protectors": Qur'an 4:34, in Ali, *The Meaning of the Holy Qur'an*, p. 195.

p. 65 "Those who surrender": Qur'an 33:35, in Lindsay, *Daily Life in the Medieval Islamic World*, p. 180.

p. 65 "Women are": Badawi, *Gender Equity in Islam*, p. 30.

p. 65 "From what is left": Qur'an 4:7, in Badawi, *Gender Equity in Islam*, p. 17.

Sources for Quotations

p. 66 "Whosoever has": Badawi, *Gender Equity in Islam*, p. 22.

p. 66 "Marriage is one half": Burckhardt, *Moorish Culture in Spain*, p. 93.

p. 66 "Actually, I accept": Badawi, *Gender Equity in Islam*, p. 23.

p. 66 "Give women": Qur'an 4:4, in Lindsay, *Daily Life in the Medieval Islamic World*, p. 183.

p. 67 "would be improper": Qur'an 4:20, in Lindsay, *Daily Life in the Medieval Islamic World*, p. 183.

p. 67 "Only the worst": Armstrong, *Muhammad*, p. 158.

p. 67 "on a footing": Qur'an 4:19, in Ali, *The Meaning of the Holy Qur'an*, p. 190.

p. 68 "Oh you who have attained": Qur'an 33:53, in Armstrong, *Muhammad*, p. 169.

p. 68 "Wives of the Prophet": Qur'an 33:32–33, in Lindsay, *Daily Life in the Medieval Islamic World*, p. 182.

p. 69 "lower their gaze": Qur'an 24:30–31, in Ali, *The Meaning of the Holy Qur'an*, p. 873.

p. 70 "sewed his clothes": Ramadan, *In the Footsteps of the Prophet*, p. 168.

p. 71 "In the name": Qur'an 1, in Esposito, *Islam*, p. 89.

p. 72 "It is permissible": Badawi, *Gender Equity in Islam*, p. 66.

p. 73 "O my Lord": Aliki Barnstone and Willis Barnstone, *A Book of Women Poets from Antiquity to Now* (New York: Schocken Books, 1980), p. 97.

p. 75 "she was already": Burckhardt, *Moorish Culture in Spain*, p. 157.

p. 75 "I recognized": ibid., p. 158.

Chapter 7

p. 77 "Behold, my prayer": Armstrong, *Muhammad*, p. 122.

p. 77 *As-salam alaykum* and *in sha Allah*: Ramadan, *In the Footsteps of the Prophet*, pp. 40 and 57.

p. 77 "Never say": Qur'an 18:23–24, in Ramadan, *In the Footsteps of the Prophet*, p. 57.

p. 78 "Whoever kills": Ramadan, *In the Footsteps of the Prophet*, p. 204.

Faith

p. 78 "Believers, when you": Qur'an 62:9–10, in Lindsay, *Daily Life in the Medieval Islamic World*, p. 145.

p. 81 "Since the Lord": Lindsay, *Daily Life in the Medieval Islamic World*, p. 164.

p. 82 "The heretic believes": Robinson, *Cambridge Illustrated History of the Islamic World*, p. 186.

p. 83 "Permission [to fight]": Qur'an 22:39, in Armstrong, *Muhammad*, p. 128.

p. 83 "Do not kill": Ramadan, *In the Footsteps of the Prophet*, p. 201.

p. 84 "If they incline": Qur'an 8:61, in Ramadan, *In the Footsteps of the Prophet*, p. 202.

p. 84 "We are back" and "It is fighting": Ramadan, *In the Footsteps of the Prophet*, p. 194.

p. 84 "Spread peace": ibid., pp. 87–88.

Index

Index

About the Author

KATHRYN HINDS grew up near Rochester, New York. She studied music and writing at Barnard College, and went on to do graduate work in comparative literature and medieval studies at the City University of New York. She has written more than thirty books for young people, including the books in the series LIFE IN ELIZABETHAN ENGLAND, LIFE IN ANCIENT EGYPT, LIFE IN THE ROMAN EMPIRE, LIFE IN THE RENAISSANCE, and LIFE IN THE MIDDLE AGES. Kathryn lives in the north Georgia mountains with her husband, their son, and an assortment of cats and dogs. In addition to writing, she is a teacher and performer of Middle Eastern dance and music, which she has been studying for twenty years. She is always learning more. Visit Kathryn online at http://www.kathrynhinds.com

About Our Consultant

DR. JOSEF W. (YOUSEF) MERI, Fellow and Special Scholar in Residence at the Royal Aal al-Bayt Institute for Islamic Thought in Amman, Jordan, has also been a visiting scholar at the American Research Centre in Egypt; the Hebrew University of Jerusalem; L'Institut Français d'Études Arabes in Damascus; the Near Eastern Studies Department at the University of California, Berkeley; and the Institute of Ismaili Studies, London. He earned his doctorate at Oxford University, specializing in medieval Islamic history and religion and in the history and culture of the Jews of the Near East. He is the author or co-author of numerous journal articles, encyclopedia entries, and books, including *The Cult of Saints Among Muslims and Jews in Medieval Syria* (Oxford: Oxford University Press, 2002), and he was general editor of *Medieval Islamic Civilization: An Encyclopedia* (New York and Oxford: Routledge, 2006).

Faith